TERROR
AND
DECORUM
POEMS
1940 - 1948

"Hush, 'tis Sir Hex, the Master of this mansion. . . .
Meseemes he'll cudgel us until we chirp.
(This happens ev'ry Spring)."

Cf. pp. 95–98

The Library of Congress has catalogued this publication as follows:

Library of Congress Cataloging in Publication Data

Viereck, Peter Robert Edwin, 1916–
    Terror and decorum: poems, 1940-1948.

    I. Title.
PS3543.I325T4 1972   811'.5'4   78-178796
ISBN 0-8371-6296-3

TERROR
AND
DECORUM

POEMS
1940 - 1948

BY

PETER VIERECK

GREENWOOD PRESS, PUBLISHERS
WESTPORT, CONNECTICUT

Grateful acknowledgment is made by the author to the following magazines and periodicals and publishers for granting permission to reprint poems which originally appeared in their pages:

"From Ancient Fangs," copyright 1947 by *Kenyon Review;* "Hard Times Redeemed by Soft Discarded Values" (under title of "Now Kindness"), copyright 1947 by *Kenyon Review;* "For Two Girls Setting Out in Life," English copyright 1947 by *Horizon* (London); North American copyright 1948 by *American Letters,* Charleston, S. C.; "Don't Look Now But Mary Is Everybody," copyright 1947 by *Partisan Review;* "The Big Graveyard," copyright 1948 by *Voices* (New York); "Kilroy" (under title of "Kilroy Was Here"), copyright 1947 by *Atlantic Monthly;* "Love Song to Eohippus," copyright 1947 by *Atlantic Monthly;* "Poet" (under title of "The Planted Poet"), copyright 1947 by *Harper's Magazine;* "You all are static; I alone am moving" (under title of "I Alone Am Moving"), copyright 1948 by *Harper's Magazine;* "Well Said, Old Mole," copyright 1947 by *Harper's Magazine;* "A Walk on Snow," copyright 1948 by *Yale Review;* "Convoy from New York" (under title of "By V-Mail to Ellen"), copyright 1943 by *The New Yorker Magazine, Inc.* (formerly the F-R Publishing Corporation); "Ode to Throne and Altar" (under title of "Ode to the M.P. Chasing Me Through a North African Town"), copyright 1944 by *The New Yorker Magazine, Inc.* (formerly the F-R Publishing Corporation); "Affirmations," copyright 1948 by *Inventario* (Florence, Paris, and London); "The Day's No Rounder than Its Angles Are," copyright 1945 by *Chimera;* "Love Poem," copyright 1945 by *Chimera;* "Love Poem" (in Italian translation by Sergio Baldi under title of "Poesia d'Amore), Italian copyright 1945 by *Il Mundo* (Florence, Italy); "American Dialogue" (in its unrevised first version), copyright 1940 by *Common Sense* (New York); "Photomontage of the Urban Parks," copyright 1947 by *Western Review* (at the University of Kansas); "Stanzas of the Old Unrest" (in longer, unrevised version), Italian copyright 1946 by *Anglica, Rivista di Studi Inglesi e Americani* (at University of Florence); "Graves Are Made to Waltz On" (in a longer, unrevised version), copyright 1940 by *Poetry* (Chicago); *"Vale* from Carthage," copyright 1947 by *Poetry;* "Six Theological Cradle-Songs" (in shorter version under title of "Five Theological Cradle-Songs"), copyright 1947 by *Poetry;* "Elegy to All Sainthood Everywhere," copyright 1948 by *Poetry;* Part II of "Crass Times Redeemed by Dignity of Souls" (under title of "A Sort of Redemption"), copyright 1948 by *Poetry;* "African Air," copy-

vi

CONTENTS

I. ANGULAR DAYS

II. SIX THEOLOGICAL CRADLE-SONGS

III. New York

IV. And This the Man That in His Study Sits

V. News from the Sixtieth Century

VI. Athos and Assisi

VII. African Campaign

VIII. Reverence

I

ANGULAR DAYS

★ 🪷 ★

"Here abstractions have contours; here flesh is wraith;
On these cold and warming stones, only solidity throws
no shadow.
(Listen, when the high bells ripple the half-light:
Ideas, ideas, the tall ideas dancing.)"

—from "Incantation" (page 82)

POET

"Toute forme créée, même par l'homme, est immortelle. Car la forme est indépendante de la matière, et ce ne sont pas les molecules qui constituent la forme."

(Baudelaire, *Mon Cœur Mis à Nu*)

1

The night he died, earth's images all came
To gloat in liberation round his tomb.
Now vengeful colors, stones, and faces dare
  To argue with his metaphor;
And stars his fancy painted on the skies
Drop down like swords
                     to pierce his too wide eyes.

2

Words that begged favor at his court in vain—
Lush adverbs, senile rhymes in tattered gowns—
  Send notes to certain exiled nouns
And mutter openly against his reign.
While rouged clichés hang out red lights again,
Hoarse refugees report from far-flung towns
That exclamation-marks are running wild
And prowling half-truths carried off a child.

3

But he lives on in Form, and Form shall shatter
  This tuneless mutiny of Matter.
His bones are dead; his voice is horribly strong.
Those famed vibrations of life's dancing dust,
Whose thrice-named pangs are "birth" and "death"
  and "lust,"
Are but the spilt iambics of his song.
Scansion of flesh in endless ebb and flow,
The drums of duty and renown's great gong—
Mere grace-notes of that living thousand-year
Tyrannic metronome whose every gear
Is some shy craftsman buried long ago.
What terror crowns the sweetness of all song?

4

What hardness leaps at us from each soft tune
And hammers us to shapes we never planned?
This was a different dying from our own.
  Call every wizard in the land—
Bell, book, and test tube; let the dark be rife
With every exorcism we command.
In vain. This death is stronger than our life.

5

In vain we drive our stakes through such a haunter
Or woo with spiced applaudings such a heart.
His news of April do but mock our Winter
Like maps of heaven breathed on window-frost
By cruel clowns in codes whose key is lost.
Yet some sereneness in our rage has guessed
That we are being blessed and blessed and blessed
When least we know it and when coldest art
  Seems hostile,
      useless,
          or apart.

6

  Not worms, not worms in such a skull
But rhythms, rhythms writhe and sting and crawl.
He sings the seasons round, from bud to snow.
And all things are because he willed them so.

THE DAY'S NO ROUNDER
THAN ITS ANGLES ARE

(for Anya)

Mere dark is not so night-like as it seems.
The night's more silken than the dark by far.
So many dark things are not night at all:
The cupboard where the cakes and poisons are;
The coffin where old men get locked in dreams
Alive, and no one hears their knocks and screams;
Shadows; and lightlessness of curtain's fall.

The night is further than the dark is far.
The night is farness, farnesses that reel.
The day is nearness, nearnesses that jar.
The day's no rounder than its angles are.
But though its angles gash you with a wound
Invisible, each night is soft and round.

The night is softer than the dark is satin.
The night is softness, softnesses that heal
The many, many gashes where you bled.
The day is loudness, loudnesses that threaten;
An evil sexton-dwarf hides in your head.
Oh where escape his bells that peal and peal?

The night is stiller than the dark is dead.

HARD TIMES REDEEMED
BY SOFT DISCARDED VALUES

1

This was the summer when the tired girls
Breathed in the parks another planet's air
And stretched like hyphens between Here and There,
Stretched and lounged and yawned on every lawn.
Then did the planet of the tired girls
Whirl from the constellation named The Fawn
(Goodbye, mild starlight of the Sign of Fawn)
And ride into the galaxy named Fangs,
Where every dew-drop like a tear-drop hangs.
This was the summer-sob of wounded girls.

2

This was the tiredness when summer's girls
Grew soft and hidden griefs like downy curls.
Then was the drowsy melody of Languish
(Goodbye, archaic waltzing-world of Languish)
Jazzed to the bad bad bad blues of Wild Anguish.
Serene old Mozart world—peace ethics laws—
Fades like girl-sighs. Or begs like kitten paws.
Or soars, unheeded like too pale a star,
Into the limbo where the tired are.
This was the faded June of fainting girls.

3

Then came the gnats who feed on sad young girls,
Winging and stinging through the gauze of dusk,
Buzzing and burning all that summer night.
Then did all perfumes bitterly take flight
Out of the stylish cloying of Sweet Musk
(Goodbye, warm pensive world of sensuous musk)
Into the dark dark dream-flower named Take Fright.
Then girls discovered that their dolls were dead,
Hollow yet lovely like those gold skins shed
When locusts molt, found on old trees by girls.

4

Now kindness (wide-eyed as the dolls of girls),
Killed and redeeming, shines from all pale girls.

Venice, 1945

FOR TWO GIRLS SETTING OUT IN LIFE

(a morality-play)

"The two young ladies separated. Juliette, who wanted to become a grand lady, how could she consent to be accompanied by a girl whose virtuous and plebeian inclinations might dishonor her social prestige? And Justine, for her part, how could she expose her good name to the companionship of a perverse creature who was looking forward to a life of vile lewdness and public debauchery? They bade each other an eternal adieu, and next morning they both left the convent."—Marquis de Sade, *Justine or The Misfortunes of Virtue*, 1791.

i

The sick man, though, had wit who thought you up.
Who can not picture you that fatal morning?
Homeless, not even knowing where you'll sup,
You sigh, "Adieu!" and ask yourselves, "What next?"
I sound like old Polonius—don't be vexed
If I give too avuncular a warning;
But having scanned your futures in a text,
I gasp at all the ways you'll be misled
(Your nuns behind you and your males ahead)
And want to save you from your author's plot.
When he says, "Follow me," you'd better not!

ii

Justine, by all means do be virtuous
But not in so provocative a fashion.
I'm being frank; please listen: solely thus
Can you elude that lamentable passion
For which your author lends his name to us.
The night he ties you down in Bondy Wood,
You'll learn what happens to the gauchely good.

iii

Yet you'll endure, Justine. Most stubbornly!
To love mankind, to preach tranquillity
To Etna or reverse a spinning planet
By bleating trustfully your Pauline tracts—
Such supernatural smugness is sheer granite:
No, not eroded by whole cataracts
Of fondlers groping through—beyond—your body
To sate in flesh the spirit's old distress
And plunge their seekings in some final sea.
Meanwhile, far off, a certain chic Grand Lady
Half-hears a voice each night (too kind for spleen)
That weeps for all her daytime wilfulness:
"Juliette! Juliette! What have you done to me?
It's I—your other self—your poor Justine."

iv

And you, Juliette: have fun while doing ill.
Be un-immaculate *while yet you may*
(I drop this hint to give the plot away).
But when you dance with sweating stable-lads
Or tired Dukes who giggle at your skill,
Don't think it's you who dance; the ghosts of gods
Who died before our oldest gods were young,
Twirl savagely in your polite salon:

That sofa where reclining comes so easy,
Is far more haunted than you'll ever guess.
Your lips raise shrines as mystic as Assisi
From whiteness they so piously caress.
O you are very wise (your playful nights,
That seem so casual, are primordial rites)
And very silly (promise me you'll stay
A pretty little girl who'll never spell
"Chthonic" nor learn her Freud too sadly well).
Last week I think I met you on Broadway.

v

Two truths, two sisters. An obsessive pair:
Serene in their unalterable rôles
Whether their frantic author flog or kiss them.
And either truth rebukes our limbo where
Girls are not Bad but merely Indiscreet,
Girls are not Good but merely Very Sweet,
And men are filed in their own filing-system
With frayed manila-folders for their souls—
Once labeled GOD'S OWN IMAGE: USE WITH
    CARE
But now reclassified as OBSOLETE.

vi

Justine! Juliette! We need you, both of you,
'Girls of mild silver or of furious gold.'
Revoke your spat; it is our own feud, too.
You smile? Yet you can bless us if you will.
And then—and then—identities unveiled,
Tall tales rehearsed and poutings reconciled—
    Two opposites will find each other
    And sob for half a day together;
For heaven and hell are childhood playmates still.

KILROY

(for John H. Finley, Jr.)

(*Editor's note:* An example of an unfaked epic spirit emerging from the war was the expression "Kilroy was here," scribbled everywhere by American soldiers and implying that nothing was too adventurous or remote.)

I

Also Ulysses once—that other war.
    (Is it because we find his scrawl
    Today on every privy door
    That we forget his ancient rôle?)
Also was there—he did it for the wages—
When a Cathay-drunk Genoese set sail.
Whenever "longen folk to goon on pilgrimages,"
Kilroy is there;
        he tells The Miller's Tale.

2

At times he seems a paranoiac king
Who stamps his crest on walls and says, "My own!"
But in the end he fades like a lost tune,
Tossed here and there, whom all the breezes sing.
"Kilroy was here"; these words sound wanly gay,
    Haughty yet tired with long marching.
He is Orestes—guilty of what crime?—
    For whom the Furies still are searching;
    When they arrive, they find their prey
(Leaving his name to mock them) went away.
Sometimes he does not flee from them in time:
"Kilroy was——"
        (*with his blood a dying man*
    Wrote half the phrase out in Bataan.)

3

Kilroy, beware. "HOME" is the final trap
That lurks for you in many a wily shape:
In pipe-and-slippers plus a Loyal Hound
      Or fooling around, just fooling around.
Kind to the old (their warm Penelope)
But fierce to boys,
               thus "home" becomes that sea,
Horribly disguised, where you were always drowned,—
      (How could suburban Crete condone
The yarns you would have V-mailed from the sun?)—
And folksy fishes sip Icarian tea.

One stab of hopeless wings imprinted your
      Exultant Kilroy-signature
Upon sheer sky for all the world to stare:
      "I was there! I was there! I was there!"

4

God is like Kilroy; He, too, sees it all;
That's how He knows of every sparrow's fall;
That's why we prayed each time the tightropes cracked
On which our loveliest clowns contrived their act.
The G. I. Faustus who was
                 everywhere
Strolled home again. "What was it like outside?"
Asked Can't, with his good neighbors Ought and But
And pale Perhaps and grave-eyed Better Not;
For "Kilroy" means: the world is very wide.
      He was there, he was there, he was there!

And in the suburbs Can't sat down and cried.

YOU ALL ARE STATIC; I ALONE AM MOVING

(a young tree addresses humanity)

You all are static; I alone am moving.
Racing beyond each planted Pullman wheel,
    I pity you and long to reel
You through my thousand outstretched ways of loving.
Are you alive at all? Can non-trees feel?

Run while I may, for at my pith gnaws Night.
The winds—these are great stacks of anchored air;
    I thresh them with my hard-pronged hair;
I jump right through them, roaring my delight.
Live while I may—run, run, no matter where.

How marvelous—if you but knew—is speed!
You all must wait; I am your overtaker.
    Striding to green from yellow acre,
I toss you Spring. Each dawn, my tendrils knead
Stars into pancake-suns like a tall baker.

Trudging towards snowtime, I could weep for hours
To think of birds, the birds I leave behind.
    Why did the God who keeps you blind,
Instead give sight and sentience to my flowers?
Black questions in my sap outwear my rind.

Humans (I almost envy you your peace)
Are free of this gnarled urge for Absolutes
    Which sweetens and saddens all my fruits,
Dragging my twigs down when I'd fly towards bliss—
While bugs and diamonds agonize my roots.

LOT'S WIFE

Only her gape (that wistfulness) still lingers:
Whiteness unsweltered by an eon's suns.
Still backwards juts the gesture's frozen bronze,
Carved by Jehovah's cataclysmal fingers.

The tiny stinging snows that tears are made of—
Intolerable compression welds them here.
How shall she cry who is herself a tear?
Her retinas hold all she is afraid of:

The towns He hates, the scene that petrifies.
These sockets cannot spill four thousand years
Of visible terror. One taut muscle veers
Just at her throat-line. All that fire is ice.

Homewards! The hopeless turn; the shy regret;
Earth's faces jammed against His windowpane.
Not glass—it's faces shatter always then.
The spindrift awe of Hart's obsessive pet

Seal; or Aeneas on the boat from Troy
Before harps cooled the arson into art;
Not Elba's but Saint Helen's Bonaparte;
Each backwards
                    inward
                              like the salt-girl's eye.

TO A SINISTER POTATO

O vast earth-apple, waiting to be fried,
Of all life's starers the most many-eyed,
What furtive purpose hatched you long ago
In Indiana or in Idaho?

In Indiana and in Idaho
Snug underground, the great potatoes grow,
Puffed up with secret paranoias unguessed
By all the duped and starch-fed Middle West.

Like coiled-up springs or like a will-to-power,
The fat and earthy lurkers bide their hour,
The silent watchers of our raucous show
In Indiana or in Idaho.

"They think us dull, a food and not a flower.
Wait! We'll outshine all roses in our hour.
Not wholesomeness but mania swells us so
In Indiana and in Idaho.

"In each Kiwanis Club on every plate,
So bland and health-exuding do we wait
That Indiana never, never knows
How much we envy stars and hate the rose."

Some doom will strike (as all potatoes know)
When—once too often mashed in Idaho—
From its cocoon the drabbest of earth's powers
Rises and is a star.
And shines.
And lours.

STANZAS OF THE OLD UNREST

1

In the garden
Where smooth pebbles are
And palm trees next to pine trees
And the many benches there,
A lawn is shining;
It is hedged in by a square.

2

In the garden
Where the cherub-statues are
And the lake is often looked at
But never with a stare,
The heads of children growing
Out of the shining lawn
Were afraid of the cities;
They were glad the cities were far.

3

But somewhere is much walking
On desolate dawns;
Somewhere are beaches,
Far from all lawns,
And the lovers the lovers
The lovers walk up and down.

4

"The world has a thousand cities;
Beware.
The world has a thousand cities,
Exactly one thousand cities,"
Warned a marble garden-child.
"And pains that nobody pities
And lonely sorcerers are there,
And birds have human voices,
And lovers are sick with love,
And the seagulls the seagulls
The seagulls are bitter and wild."

5

In the garden
Where breezes and benches are kind,
Where grave-eyed heads are growing
But never threateningly,
The mildest head asked sadly,
"For the sake of her eyes and her hair,
To where cities and beaches are,
Why are you going?"

The garden shivered suddenly in all its roots.

6

"New eyes new hair
Have changed you so,
Now you must go.
Now you must be
Where waters are,"
Said the gentlest statue there.
"Now you will sometimes walk
Where gulls talk."

Viale dell'Aranciera,
Borghese Gardens, Rome, 1944

THE BIG GRAVEYARD

"Not so deep as a well nor so wide as a church-door;
but 'tis enough, 'twill serve."—*Romeo and Juliet*. III, 1

She is the noon for whom the ewes increase,
The sun the yule-logs promised to the snows.
She is the stairway to and out of birth.
She is the lap and tremor of our earth.
She is a wound named Eros-Thanatos.

She is the June for whom the daughters bloom,
The twilight when the lilacs open up.
The carpet softness where the hungry drop.
The last embrace where all the travelers stop.
The warm, the waiting, the unlonely room.

In this cocoon the stars renew their wings
And bruise the welkin like a burning broom.
Of love the flesh, of loveliness the soul,
She is the calyx of all petaled things,
The cave to whom all tired whirlwinds crawl.

She is the dune where ruins and plumes are white;
They fade all night, the stones and feathers fall,
They palely fall on beds of whiter sand
That holds them all the night like a kind hand
(All night, all night till every fever cools).

All night she is the tune that lures to pools,
The dying moon to whom the ewes escape.
She is the Lilith every Adam mourns,
The living noon whose tulip gapes with peace—
But soon the war for whom the rams lock horns.

But soon: the tomb whose two lips gape.

LOVE POEM

We are the satraps of a sinking season.
Our year's a Ferris wheel, whose guests we are.
Before I rise again, I must fall far.

But not with you. Our snow-time aches with treason,
At wheel's deep dip when soil gapes nearest bone.
Then you'll stand up,
                    force doors,
                                fall out alone.

II

SIX THEOLOGICAL CRADLE-SONGS

(FOR JOHN-ALEXIS ON HIS
FIRST BIRTHDAY)

★ ★

PROÖIMION

Evil and Easter steer this star, rash babe.
Foul fellow He who dolve so strait a glebe.
Fey fellow He who died for such daft globe.
Woe worth the mime who be thy astrolabe.

Though woxe a wight so stout as oaken wood,
Sware he by Mahound—or by Godis rood,
Cowl-clad—or clipt more doxies than he wed,
Him felled swart axman that more stoutly hewed.
. . . Ho Carpenter! wilt resurrect smit wood?

Newcomer, reck no rede but this, perfay:
Thy masque below hight "Love and Wellaway"
(Certës, withouten both were nary play).
Then strut thy buskins; sigh but strut them gay.

Boy, stand too proud for chapmen when they prate.
(Or carl or younker, equally askew.)
'Tis mummers, mummers do delight Jesú.
Only the gleeman glegly ogles Fate.

Foul fellow lispeth sweet but drinketh gore.
Fey fellow He who drank vile vinegar;
For love of thee, He gat Him thorny gear;
He gat scant dayspring for the dawn He bare.

Twain fellows have and halve the soul of thee;
Sic boon and bane hath each nativity.
Nurses and Furies trim each fledgling-tree.
And I: as mime.

　　　　　　　And in thy pate all three.

I. BETTER COME QUIETLY

(a nursery jingle)

Baby John: O kinsfolk and gentlefolk, PLEASE be for-
giving,
But nothing can lure me to living, to living.
I'm snug where I am; I don't WISH to burst
through.
Chorus of Nurses, Furies, & Muses: That's what YOU
think. If only you KNEW!

Baby John: Well then YES, I'll be BORN, but my EARTH
will be heaven;
My dice will throw nothing but seven-eleven;
Life is tall lilacs, all giddy with dew.
Chorus of Nurses, Furies, & Muses: That's what YOU
think. If only you KNEW!

Baby John: Well then YES, there'll be sorrows, be sorrows
that best me;
But these are mere teasings to test me, to test
me.
We'll ZOOM from our graves when God
orders us to.
Chorus of Nurses, Furies, & Muses: That's what YOU
think. If only you KNEW!

Baby John: Well then YES, I'll belie my belief in survival.
But IF there's no God, then at least there's no
devil:
If at LAST I must die—well, at LEAST when
I do,
It's clear I won't sizzle.
Chorus of Nurses, Furies, & Muses: If only you KNEW!

24

II. A HEALTHY OUTLOOK

(common sense from Seth the Defiler)

My name is air; come strut on me.
When you've TRUTH's bad penny, pass it.
Best cure for what pale scribes are after
   Is boisterous laughter.
Useful, too, is Prussic acid.

My name is fire; play with me.
When you've LOVE's bad penny, pass it.
Best cure for what sick girls are after
   Is sultry laughter.
Just as sweet is Prussic acid.

My name is water; write on me.
When you've ART's bad penny, pass it.
Best cure for what quaint dreams are after
   Is cackling laughter.
If this won't work, try Prussic acid.

My name is quicksand; build on me.
When you've GOD's bad penny, pass it.
Best cure for what His saints are after
   Is secret screaming laughter.
Safest cure is Prussic acid.

III. WHY CAN'T I LIVE FOREVER?

"Here comes a candle to light you to bed,
And here comes a chopper to chop off your head."
                                        (*Nursery rhyme*).

DEATH is a blind flamingo, hunting fishes.
He does not mean to gobble you or me—
And when his beak swings wildly, never wishes
To scare us so. If only he could see!

At night he wades through surf to seek a mate.
That's why he stinks of salt and oyster shells.
It is his blindness keeps him celibate:
This bungler thinks he kisses when he kills.

I wish he wouldn't make us die. I wish
He'd spread his wings one night and fly away
To higher planets for his girls and fish.
But he's got used to Earth
                            and plans to stay.

IV. BLINDMAN'S BUFF

Night-watchmen think of dawn and things auroral.
Clerks wistful for Bermudas think of coral.
The poet in New York still thinks of laurel.
(But lovers think of death and touch each other
As if to prove that love is still alive.)

The Martian space-crew, in an Earthward dive,
Think of their sweet unearthly earth Up There,
Where darling monsters romp in airless air.
(Two lovers think of death and touch each other,
Fearing that day when only one's alive.)

We think of cash, but cash does not arrive.
We think of fun, but fate will not connive.
We never mention death. Do we survive?
(The lovers think of death and touch each other
To live their love while love is yet alive.)

Prize-winners are so avid when they strive;
They race so far; they pile their toys so high.
Only a cad would trip them. Yet they die.
(The lovers think of death and touch each other;
Of all who live, these are the most alive.)

When all the lemming-realists contrive
To swim—where to?—in life's enticing tide,
Only a fool would stop and wait outside.
(The lovers stop and wait and touch each other.
Who twinly think of death are twice alive.)

Plump creatures smack their lips and think they thrive;
The hibernating bear, but half alive,
Dreams of free honey in a stingless hive.
He thinks of life at every lifeless breath.
(The lovers think of death.)

27

V. GAME CALLED ON ACCOUNT OF
DARKNESS

Once there was a friend.
He watched me from the sky.
Maybe he never lived at all.
Maybe too much friendship made him die.

When the gang played cops-and-robbers in the alley,
It was my friend who told me which were which.
Now he doesn't tell me any more.
(Which team am I playing for?)

My science teacher built a telescope
To show me every answer in the end.
I stared and stared at every star for hours.
I couldn't find my friend.

At Sunday school they said I breathe too much.
When I hold my breath within the under
Side of earth, they said I'll find my friend.
. . . I wonder.

He was like a kind of central-heating
In the big cold house, and that was good.
One by one I have to chop my toys now,
As firewood.

Every time I stood upon a crossroads,
It made me mad to feel him watch me choose.
I'm glad there's no more spying while I play.
Still, I'm sad he went away.

VI. HIDE AND SEEK

(an Easter ballad)

"Come OUT, come OUT, wherEVer you are,"
The frisking children chorused.
    When playtime ends,
    All hidden friends
Are bound to come out of the forest.

"Come OUT, come OUT, wherEVer you are,"
The tidy children chorused,
    In the short proud street
    Where our lives are neat
On the nearer side of the forest.

"Come OUT, come OUT, wherEVer you are,"
The puzzled children chorused.
    When fun is over,
    Why doesn't the rover
Come whooping out of the forest?

"Come OUT, come OUT, wherEVer you are,"
The lonely children chorused;
    For the greater the dark
    The less the lark
When you wait till dusk near a forest.

"Come OUT, come OUT, wherEVer you are,"
The shivering children chorused.
    (With some wonderful toy
    Can't we tug back the boy
Who is westering into the forest?)

"Come OUT, come OUT, wherEVer you are,"
We aging children chorused—
    While beyond our shout
    A boy comes out
On the farther side of the forest.

III

NEW YORK

"It was the lark, the herald of the morn,
No nightingale."

(Romeo and Juliet, III, 5)

WHAT A PRETTY NET

Where do the garlands and the garbage go?
The night-wind knows. A peeping Tom, he'll know
You all, New Yorkers, know each snore and prayer
And what you draped across that bedside chair.

There's no wind like him; breathed in dangerous doses,
He'll tweak at heart-cores, leaving in his train
The fashionable Fifth Avenue neuroses,
The muggings in some scorned and scornful lane.

He blows, with lewd side-glances, through Bronx Park
The secret scents and giggles of its dark.
Then, yawning, to Manhattan docks he sweeps
Dawn's fog and, curled up in an ash-can, sleeps.

But you, New York, shall never sleep nor rest
While two Gods fish for you, your holy pair.
Their net of nerves and subways has been cast;
Your five trapped boroughs gasp like trout in air.

You kiss the net in sweet hypnotic trance;
Goddess and God draw tight round you Their mesh:
Hysteria, always straining at Her leash,
And Profit with His jitterbugs at dance.

DON'T LOOK NOW
BUT MARY IS EVERYBODY

Mary, long by Boss's kisses bored,
Quit desk and stole His yacht and jumped aboard.
Her lamb took she, for purer were his kisses.
Compass and pistol took she in her purse.
Free sailed she north to eat new freedom up.
And her helped ocean and grew calm and snored.
But when with bleating chum she cuddled up,
Unleashed His typhoons Boss; therein no bliss is.
Then knew she—by four signs—whose jig was up:

Her buoyed the life-preserver down, not up;
True was the pistol's aim, but in reverse;
The compass steered, but only toward abysses;
The little lamb nipped Mary's thighs and roared.

ALWAYS TO LOVE YOU, AMERICA,
ALWAYS TO FIGHT YOU

"New York ain't America"—ancient proverb

AMERICA:

Don't think I haven't watched you. There's a cure
For towns too un-American.
Don't think I'll let some alien hurricane
Blow down the fence that keeps my suburbs pure.

NEW YORK:

Your forests now are fences, and of late
You talk less of "frontiers" and more of real estate.
That's boring to the unseen spirit-throng
Of dancers—laughing south of right and wrong—
Whose footsteps groove the patterns of our fate
And whom it's dangerous to bore for long.

AMERICA:

I know you; you were always my stab-in-the-back,
Doubter at picnics, drugstore heretic.
You were always the stowaway
Who wouldn't go away;
Already that time on the *Mayflower*
When I was the psalm the captain read
To all the Fine Folks overhead,
You were the dirty joke below the deck.

NEW YORK:

I have a child named *Dagokikeandmick*.
You wouldn't play with her when she was sick.

35

AMERICA:
Such white-hot coals were stoking such dark eyes.

NEW YORK:
I showed her younger names to make her well.
And now her name is *Future*. Better tell
Your angel-Saxons and your Anglo-nice.

AMERICA:
Love me! I'll give you half my paradise:
A deepfreeze disinfected liberty.

NEW YORK:
But . . . when throats are shrill for bread . . .

AMERICA:
Let 'em eat the Statue of Liberty.

NEW YORK:
You talk of liberty but mean your bread.
I talk of bread but mean
That hate of hate, that love for new-world love,
All the fierce foolishness between
Immigrants' eyes when they half gape, half scoff
At what you built in my harbor in front of me.
Not bread, yet good to see.

AMERICA:
And if I try it? If our kids run off,
Bending in cornfields, budgeting in slums?
Their heir—what must our heir do when he comes?

NEW YORK:
Destroy.
An angry ditch-digger, he'll clear
Our miles for certain unseen deathless feet
Till even you can hear
Their dance through Forty-Second Street,
Through my too rapid jive their terrible ripening joy.

AMERICA:
Launched on the upswing of that whirlwind time,
The asphalt bonfire my prairies hated so
Will rise—Times Square above America?—

NEW YORK:
Rise past your Rockies, scrape Pike's Peak, outclimb
McKinley—America a thousand years below—
And, hovering like sheer height itself, will glow
Midnight geometries
Of snowflake flawlessness
Where "love" and "law," by pattern reconciled, must rhyme.

AMERICA:
Lighting my provinces, lighting my prejudice,
Lugging what hides:
Flow of my discontent,
Ebb of my continent,
Times Square, moon of my tides.

NEW YORK:
With rebel compasses,
Then let us trace our own astronomies,
Too high, too healing for these disputations.
Earths live or die
By all the fullnesses
They build and build into an empty sky.

AMERICA:

Risky . . . where you would tug me to.
Your friends, who dance us, might in their impatience—

NEW YORK:

Let's hurry, for our acorn days are few.

AMERICA:

You ambush history with a mugger's leap
And rave of hedgeless worlds that make my suburbs weep.
A shyster's slickness with a mystic's heart,
Jazz-jittery nerves but true
Trigger-finger, that's your part:
To do gods' dirty work. But after you—

STIFLING OF HEARTS
A HUNDRED TIMES A DAY

Sometimes a waitress laughing from a window,
To plates a truant and with comet's hair,
Enchants his snakes of longing like a Hindu
Till they sway anciently and learn *la chair*
Est triste.
A tryst?

But plates need slaves: *la chère*
Est triste, and now from window back to table
All hips strut out of sight and into fable
With Helen's scorn—and Cinderella's prayer.

HOMILY ON THE PIETY
OF ALL HERD ANIMALS

(a Mammoth idyll)

I

You pilgrims of the Rural Myth who flee
New York,
             come home, come home again, and see
What pastoral still soothes the Age of Smoke:
Theocritus now hymns a metal flock—

"Fifth Avenue Buses," iron-skinned yet mild
(Tame fire-puffers who would not singe a child),
Cowering low-roofed calves and towering bulls,
Grazing America's Arcadian hills.

2

As some lost troll might stumble on the lair
Of sleeping dragons
                     and might stare and stare
And marvel that their snores made mountains shake
And run away on tiptoe lest they wake,

So now by chance I find the warehouse sheds
Where tired buses doze in secret beds,
From all New York as artfully concealed
As elephant graveyards in the Congo weald.

3

You sleep! May Muses bless each dreaming wheel,
Rhymed quatrains of Manhattan's song-in-steel,
And bless your fenders, staunch as tusks in rage,
Heroic couplets
                    on an asphalt page.

O noble brutes whose honor is: "We serve,"
Your crooning engines nurse our every nerve
With patient, gawky love through urban stress.
Such heavy ever-bungled kindliness

Implies not sleekness but sheer shagginess:
Riderless once in your young Ice Age time,
MAMMOTHS,
                    turned equine for a single dime.

4

More chivalrous than subways and more silent,
Green double-decker landmarks of our island,
Big loyal lopers, through our soot and rain
You lumber out
                    in pious herds
                                        each dawn.

Then scatter far on separate lonely treks,
Then here at midnight huddle flank to flank.
And now you sleep! Lest rusty squeaks should vex
Your well-earned peace, may every spring relax;

May gulps and gulps of oil bless every thirsty tank!

LOVE SONG TO EOHIPPUS

(Dictionary definition: "EOHIPPUS, Greek for dawn-horse, small graceful prehistoric ancestor of modern equine family; size of rabbit; had four toes, no hoofs.")

I

Dance, dance in this museum case,
Ballet-star of our mammal race,
Attar and avatar of grace.

2

Sweet Eohippus, "dawn horse" in
   That golden Attic tongue which now
      Like you and Helen is extinct,
Like Cheshire cat of fading grin,
   Like Carthage and like Villon's snow,
      With death and beauty gently linked.

3

Yet all are deathless in their fashion:
   You live in science, they in song,
      You in museums, she in Homer.
She cannot help but live while passion
   Still lives; your dancing lives as long
      As grace; "extinct" is a misnomer.

4

Because sly Darwin liked the Fit
  And Mendel, good gray monk, sowed peas,
    Dame Evolution said benignly,
"My child, get bigger," and you did;
  "Look here, those silly toes must cease!",
    And you grew hoofs and frisked equinely.

5

When you were dodging dinosaurs
  So recklessly, they were gigantic;
    But look how Nature turns the tables:
Now they, who scared you with their roars,
  Have changed to lizards, wee and frantic,
    And you're immense and live in stables.

6

Ballet-star of our mammal race,
Last lingering of earth's first grace,
Dance on in this museum case.

GENTLE SONG

Through Algiers Rome New York across two wars,
Love, my first waiting I do still recall:

The little boy was waiting in the rain,
Hoping those footsteps might blaze past again
Which made the street a milky way of stars.
And though that night his wait was all in vain,
Whom could his poems, had he found you, call?
Who, having won you, needs to dream at all?

Now you are names and faces ever new,
And still his songs are wistfulness for you.
From which horizon and by what sun's rise,
Ever-awaited beautiful cold faces,
Will you at last dawn day-bright to his eyes,
That have but seen your half-seen twilight traces?

LOOK, HART, THAT HORSE
YOU RIDE IS WOOD

(H. C., 1899–1932)

i

Above the River that is East,
Perched on the highest stair,
Though he did not budge from Brooklyn Bridge,
He sauntered toward Saint-Terre.

>   (*Hart, Hart, can you hear me?*
>   *Hey Hart, don't jump!*)

In Dago town, in Chinatown,
In any old bazaar,
Through the folklore path of let's-make-myth
He sauntered toward Saint-Terre.

>   (*Can't you hear me, Hart, can't you hear me?*
>   *Hart, Hart, don't jump!*)

For love of sails and sailors,
For any gleam of bar,
Though he seemed to go to Mexico,
He sauntered toward Saint-Terre.

ii

A Holy Land's a nowhere land;
        Ohio's everywhere.
Look, Hart, that horse you ride is wood.
Can wheels say more than Chaucer could,
        Hick gaper at Times Square?

45

(Hart, Hart, can you hear me?
Hey Hart, don't jump!)

Daddy's clerks were daddy's spies
    In that Cleveland candy store:
"And if you catch Hart scribbling verses——."
He fled that middling-west, with curses,
    For Saint-Manhattanterre.

(Can't you hear me, Hart, can't you hear me?
Hart, Hart, don't jump!)

Was freedom merely this: to flee
    Nine years from selling fudge?
Would gorgeous lies bring freedom quicker?
Walt did it—Walt, the city slicker,
    Sold Hart the Brooklyn Bridge.

(Hart, Hart, can you hear me?
Hey Hart, don't jump!)

Straight to the island that is east
    He sauntered, and he found
New York was the clerks his daddy hired
Plus gin plus sea; then Hart felt tired,
    Drank both and drowned.

PHOTOMONTAGE OF THE URBAN PARKS

Though birds can flee when colors scorch like embers,
The lawns lie trapped below in fire and frost and dark.
Image of love in all love's fierce Novembers:
A burning oak-leaf in a shivering park.

But even in cities: Pan. Or was it Francis?
Then parks, all parks, lunge free and flood our eyes.
Vengeful return of disestablished fancies:
A live kaleidoscope of fireflies.

Birds are exploding into bloom and glowing,
And petals fan our sleep with little wings.
(Into our eardrums what glass snake is flowing?
It is a Moorish fountain, and it sings.)

Stalactites raping soft moss grottoes. Shouting
Ducks from Bronx Park on Oxford swan-ponds floating.
Versailles and Schoenbrunn, waltzing knee to knee,
Elope into the eighteenth century.

All spins and mixes. Who cried, "Stop!"? Alarms
Won't help now. Faster. Whirlwind, whirl again
A park called Eden, Francis *with* Saint Pan:
The white snow with the rainbow in her arms.

IV

AND THIS THE MAN
THAT IN HIS STUDY SITS

"Poets and pipers and such peevish cattle"

(Stephen Gosson, 1579)

"He surfeits upon curséd necromancy;
Nothing so sweet as magic is to him,
Which he prefers before his chiefest bliss:
And this the man that in his study sits."

(Marlowe)

DOLCE OSSESSIONE

Will no one watch me? Look!, I'll dance on thread
Or hold my breath for cameras till I burst.
Step close, please; see, I'll pick your pockets first
And shine—like truth?, like lies?—and then drop dead.
Pathfinder, poacher, voodoo god, and quack:
My names, unending as an almanac,
Spin round me like a madman's spelling-bee.
I am the prodigal who won't come back;

Phobic of wheels, I'll hide beneath the sea.

The sea! What beast existences I'll choose!
At first I'll curl in wombs of shells and doze
For years and years in tepid, crooning dark.
I'll urge Obsession on: an eel, I'll swim
To every far Sargasso of my whim.
When I hear bathers laugh, I'll be a shark.

A flame-scaled trout, I'll shimmer through your nets—
Like lies?, like truth?—and gasp on fatal sands.
Trailed fawning by lascivious hungry cats,
What child will scoop me up,
                                        what pudgy hands?

A WALK ON SNOW

I

Pine-trail; and all the hours are white, are long.
But after miles—a clearing: snow and roundness.
Such circle seemed a rite, an atavism,
A ripple of the deep-plunged stone of Myth.
I crossed that ring to loiter, not to conjure.
Stood in the center as in melodrama.
Wondered: if this center were a gate?
A gate from earth to non-earth? Gate where fingers,
Where rays perhaps, are fumbling signals through?
    Or are stars cold for all their brightness,
Deaf to our urgencies as snowflakes are?
Then magic blazed: a star spoke through the gate:
"I am not cold; I am all warm inside."

2

At once new longing charged and shook the air
Like spreading tremors of a storm's spilt moan.
Star-tunes lured old tellurian lonelinesses.
Like chord-joined notes of one sky-spanning octave,
Orbs blent in universal tremolo.
    "Star, star, reachable star!
Truly," I called, "you are all warm inside."
Shy through the gate came answer, frail in space:
"Good luck, brother. It's not so far across."

3

Being absurd as well as beautiful,
Magic—like art—is hoax redeemed by awe.
(Not priest but clown, the shuddering sorcerer
Is more astounded than his rapt applauders:
"Then all those props and Easters of my stage
Came true? But I was joking all the time!")
Art, being bartender, is never drunk;
And magic that believes itself, must die.
My star was rocket of my unbelief,
Launched heavenward as all doubt's longings are;
     It burst when, drunk with self-belief,
I tried to be its priest and shouted upward:
"Answers at last! If you'll but hint the answers
For which earth aches, that famous Whence and **Whither**;
Assuage our howling Why with final fact."

4

At once the gate slammed shut, the circle snapped,
The sky was usual and broad and silent.
A snowflake of impenetrable cold
Fell out of sight incalculably far.
Ring all you like, the lines are disconnected.
Knock all you like, no one is ever home.
(Unfrocked magicians freeze the whole night long;
Holy iambic can not thaw the snow
They walk on when obsessive crystals bloom.)
Shivering I stood there, straining for some frail
Or thunderous message that the heights glow down.
     I waited long; the answer was
The only one earth ever got from sky.

BALLAD OF THE JOLLIE GLEEMAN

(a parable for songcraft—or haplie politicke)

High thanes and highborn ladies, stay and heed
An ambling gleeman sore athirst for mead.
I chaunt a rime whose end will stound you all;
On sward nor sea, its like ye'll never hear.
No overweener I but tuneful thrall,
A lackpelf glad to babble for his beer.

(tuneth cithern and commenceth;
bawcocks and damoizels daunce winsomelie together)

A dragon-worm did bogey all the East.
From pilgrims plump he gat him bonnie feast.
He wrake his wrath on them, atop a wrack
Of saunterers who saunterer never back.
He gouged, he gored, he thwarted every thwack.
Atop twelve skulls did smirk yon shameless Beast.

A pure Crusader, pricking to Seint Terre,
Did meet yon godless worm, flesh-gorging there.
With splendid spleen our Hero's eyën shone;
He clave that worm unto the neckë-bone;
He drave his swingle till it swisht the air.
Hell's henchman wallopt he in his own lair.

(poureth self jug of mead and quaffeth)

Pax bless such sword-playe, bless Seint George's dreame!
Pox blight them all that playe not on God's teame!
Scathers and skulkers, doers in the dark,
Each werewolf (grislie guest with baleful bark),
Each Thing that poppeth out from under stones:
Grace graunt them all such sore-nickt neckë-bones.

> (*shuddereth righteouslie; damoizels, while dauncing
> wantonlie, make sign of true cross with their fans*)

Out tript a princess, blanche as moonës dew,
Imprisond in yon dragon's swart purlieu.
More sheen her tress than Troytown ever knew;
More sheer her dress than spider's treachrous fleece,
Thro which did beck and keek her dimplie knees.
Her paps were pippins such as Eden grew

To Adam's bane whan did befall that Fall
From which disgrace may Grace redeeme us all.
(Withouten Grace no soul is tuppence worth,
As hell-folk wot; their groans give pleasaunt mirth
To gentle Seints above.) For love of Grace
Our Hero holp yon helpless love-ripe lass.

> (*wipeth brow and eke filleth new jug; courtiers toss
> him coins and yawn*)

For love of her, he dropt both shield and sword.
(To breach sic maidenhead were goodlie sport.)
With dapper dirk she breached our Hero's side;
"Quaint thanks thou gavest me," he sulkt—and died.
But she—"sweet Fiend, sweet ghastlie worm!" she cried.
(Praise Grace, whose ways we ken not but record.)

In pain her loathlie lord his claws did flail.
Soft swaddled she his sore-nickt neckë-bone
And, crooning, nurst her dank dark leman hale;
Then, hand in paw, they clomb his ancient throne.
Atop such pile of skulls as sought the Grail,
Beautie and Beast once more made amorous moan.

> (*unstringeth cithern and draineth jug; then locketh
> gate while bowing reverentlie*)

Now is yon arch-worm Earl of all the East.
So droll a tale, I ween ye never wist.
Ye've had your song, and I—I'll have my feast
> (*removeth jollie mask and revealeth monstrous jaws*)
On all of you. Yon Fiend whereof I sing
> (*groweth mountain-high*)
Is your poor bard. Too late to scape my fang!
Now, daintie lordlings, daunce your final fling.

TO A VEGETARIAN LIVING AS PURE SPIRIT

"und von dem niedren Fleisch der Tiere rein"

You whose clean guts are free from passion's pains
And from the sultry meat of quadruped:
The sweet juice shining through your wrist's blue veins
Would taste like lotus nectar if it bled.

Lucent your skin, like wings of princess-ants.
When sunflowers go to sleep, your head droops too,
For sunset lugs them both. Coy moss peeps through
Your chin like beard, as green as all your plants.

Your clothes wilt like sick petals while you sit
On toadstool thrones; your toes sprout roots in clover.
The dragonflies, big-eyed and striped all over,
Sing just for you; they know your joy in it.

At will, your mask is Buddha: there you squat!
At will, you are a timeless temple-vase
While meat-hunters, who roar and copulate,
Race deathward till their eager eyeballs glaze.

And when we caper round you to entice
Your poise into the somersaults of lust,
You shake your head so sadly that your sighs
Float like pink clouds above our heavy dust.

You'll sit for eons and for eons so,
More pure each eon and more subtly mincing
Till even a falling moonbeam's unfelt blow
Martyrs your forehead into unseen wincing.

THE FOUR STAGES OF CRAFTSMANSHIP

1

Ghost haunts your sleeping all the night.
Ghost walks behind you all day long.
Ghost likes to goad you into song—
But halts your hand when you would write.

Your blows can never make it weep,
And all your jokes can't make it talk.
Better walk quickly when you walk.
Better sleep lightly when you sleep.

2

The parliament of silences—
Where whatever might be, is—
Judges each word I thought I built so well.
Each time, pride asks: "O Inexpressible,
Does not this new word KNOW
What silence looks like?"
                    Echo answers: "NO."

3

(*"je hais le mouvement qui déplace les lignes"—Baudelaire*)

Harsh hammer hardens my
Clay sullenness to stone mourning:
Rightly enraged under a sunless sky,
A wise hate on a wan morning.

Give up too much and you give just enough
To spin what shines.
Will words most silk from deeds most rough
Trap life in lines?

4

What makes him different seems so small a thing:
His knack of shaping joy from pain by rime.
He whittles joy so sharp it is a spear
And jabs it deep between the ribs of time.
Even his sickness blesses; singers wear
Neurosis like new roses when they sing.

IN THE DESTRUCTIVE ELEMENT IMMERSE

The hoodoo rodents of love's submarine
Are much too gray. Are publicly obscene.
No paws that burrow like love's submarine
Are furrier than certain waves have been;
But waves!—but like a gesture of abhorrence
Their corrugation rolls from love in torrents.

No minks that slither like love's submarine
Have pelts more glossy than the sea is sheen;
But sea!—it spews, it sheds these gray pollutions
By always beaching love, their carrier.
Spiraling down and up through brine and air,
Love's valves become involved in convolutions;
And all descent is gray.
                    But rich.
                    But rare.

V

NEWS FROM THE SIXTIETH CENTURY

★ ✾ ★

"It may be, as certain philosophers maintain, that the
air is peopled with spirits, who foresee future events
and—out of pity—warn mankind."

(Machiavelli, *Discourses*)

"Altogether no-good number-one big-fella wind,
Him bugger-up finish small-fella flower.
This fella summer
By-'n'-by him finish quicktime."

(Shakespeare, sonnet xviii)*

*"Rough winds do shake the darling buds of May,
And Summer's lease hath all too short a date"—
as recited in Pidgin English by a cannibal schoolmaster of the Solomon
Islands, on being asked his view of the future. (Recorded by skipper
Howard Hugo, the wellknown explorer, translator, and musician.)

61

FROM ANCIENT FANGS

(the time of this poem is in the far future, shortly
after peace and love return to earth)

i

Like lamp of intricate stained-glass which hangs
    From curved blue ceiling,
A fat bright-bellied insect hangs up there.
    At night, on traveler,
It drops like rich and heavy poison welling
    From ancient fangs.

ii

That insect's not the only thing which falls.
So many things must fall in their short day.
Careers and wine-cups; bombs and tennis-balls.
Even the sun. But sky? The sky must stay.

But now the sky itself is caving in.
O good old sky, O lid that keeps us snug,
Dear blue in which we always used to trust
As in the nurse our childhood bullied so,
When comfort was to see her loyal grin,
Ugly and safe, beam down on us below:
Dear sky, we pray to you, hold on, you must!
Hold tighter, sky. Be roof to us, not rug.

"It seems I'm being prayed to; I
   Am sky,
Older than hours and than miles more far,
   Your spectator.
When worlds grow honest, noble, clean, or clever,
   I fall and smother them forever.
To keep your high roof high, stop being good.
   All sights bore Me now but blood.
The main thing is to kill. And kill. And kill.
   First with your Springfield. Then with steel.

And when steel breaks, with hands and stumps of hands.
And when you've killed all strangers, kill your friends.
And if you've used up humans, stone a rat.
Call it a whim—I like My world like that.
It's your world, too. The only world you'll get."

"At school they never used to talk like You."
   "No, not like Me."
"People back home don't want such things to do."
   "Perhaps. We'll see."
"Men won't splash harmless blood just for Your thirst."
   "No, not at first."

CHILD OF THE SIXTIETH CENTURY

His parents poisoned each other the same night.
His brothers strangled each other in the lilac garden.
He never sang songs at all; before he learnt words,
The nurse he loved most was paid to rip out his tongue.

Then all the Elders held court against him in Christ Park;
Then conscripts forgot to bow before him on Green Hill;
Then all his five overlord-nations leagued against him.
His flight at twelve. His exile. And soon his home-coming,

With the far-off foreign barbarians whom he had trained to
Such hardness that they sobbed like girls with delight
To watch him, their darling, be even harder than they.
After their famous right wing breached the flank at Boar
    Fells,

Maps called Christ Park the Desert of Elderly Skulls;
Widows renamed Green Hill the Swamp of Red Mud;
Historians knew his five proud overlord-nations
As slaves of the slaves of slaves. On his eighteenth birth-
    day—

"No longer harder than we now, merely more cruel,"
Grumbled his chosen, his foreign-faced guards, who in
    secret
Returned to their native forbidden dialect-songs.
Then light was his sleep and heavy the armor he slept in.

But no, it did not happen; it never did;
No hand quite touched him, always he was faster;
And the clumsy hairy hands and the deft and soft
Were hacked from wrists like twigs that hindered his
strolling.

And when at twenty he died, it was from within,
At banquet, all from within, by his own blood stifled,
His delicate blood, too rich and ancestor-spiced.
Then how astounded all were, even the cynics,

(O this was the sixtieth cycle), at such a queer ending:
The only lord-child they knew who had lived until twenty,
The first human being in four thousand years who had died
Neither screaming and charred to black by the fire of foes

Nor swollen and soggy, suddenly drowned by his friends.

FOR AN ASSYRIAN FRIEZE

"I, the great king, the powerful king, king of the
world, King of Assyria, the king whose path was a
cyclone, whose battle was a flaming sea, I am powerful, all-powerful, exalted, almighty, majestic, all-im-
portant in power."—inscription of 670 B.C.

Sometimes a lion with a prophet's beard
Lopes from a bas-relief to stretch his claws.
His bestial eyes are wonderfully sad.

Then he grows wings, the terrible king grows wings,
And flies above the black Euphrates loam,
Hunting for enemies of Nineveh.

His names are Shamshi and Adádnirari,
Tiglath-Piléser, Assurbanipal,
And the first Sargon of Dur-Shárukin.

*"The day my chariots stormed the town, I waxed
My beard with oil of rose and waterlily,
And freed nine pearl-caged nightingales, and built*

A pillar of skulls so high it stabbed the sun."
(Was that the tomb's voice, or the desert-wind's?
Or ours?—what ghost is still our roaring priest?)

The scribes shall say: his will outflew his wisdom.
The saints shall say: his was the sin of pride.
The skulls say nothing. And the lizards grin.

This is the rapture that the Gentiles feared
When Joshua made music masterful.
Each sinew is a harp-string crouched to twang.

The treble of such bloodlust if he pounced
Would shriek an anti-social kind of beauty
Like parrots in a gypsy carnival.

Then back to stone. In stone he sleeps the least.
It's not with love his brooding glitters so.
Earth spawns no gangrene half so luminous

As the contagion of those molten eyes.

PRINCE TANK

"That one, faroff, divine event
Towards which the whole creation moves"—Tennyson.

"And what rough beast, its hour come round at last,
Slouches towards Bethlehem to be born?"—Yeats.

I

During the fourth and fifth world wars, the tanks
Will still obey, still seem to serve their humans.
Like dinosaurs, tank corpses clog earth's swamp.
The sixth war, they will serve more sullenly—
And suddenly will *know* their day has come,
The birthday of the Prince of all the tanks,
The day the Prince of all the tanks is born.

2

Seeking with burning eyes and Christmas awe
The humblest scrap-heap of discarded tanks
In Pennsylvania's "Steel Works, Bethlehem,"
Three trim clean airmen, loosed from madhouse cells,
Will follow in a very modern airplane
A bitter, barren, bright and lying star
The day the Prince of all the tanks is born,
The birthday of the Prince of all the tanks.

3

The God-machine, the tank-who-thinks, is born.
Waking with rusty yawns that shake the planet,
The strength-which-thinks within Him knows: "I'm
    strong."
He'll grow and blot the moon out with His growth.
He'll clank with rage, a sullen moody pasha,
His boredom thirsting for the Dance of Grapes.
Then tanks will know, "Our bored young master rages,"
The day the Prince of all the tanks is born.

4

And they will dance; the tanks, the tanks will dance
On every battlefield and factory-town,
Plodding in awkward, sullen, clanking rhythm,
Treading a red and warm and salty must.
And then will humans all be jitterbugs,
Migrate like locusts from their dance-hall doors,
And sing with insect-voices metal-shrill:
"Our God is born!" and roll to Him like grapes
Till all their frenzy begs His metal treads:
"Love us to death, love us to death," the day
Creation's final goal, Prince Tank, is born.

GRAVES ARE MADE TO WALTZ ON

(From a lecture: "And so we observe with satis-
faction how modern man, by a hard-won decorous
correctness, buries all his horrid atavisms safely in
the subconscious.")

Tunes fainter on winds waywarder than others
When from the frozen marsh the wicked crystals glow,
Lure us to our disowned deep-buried banished brothers,
Who pound hot fists against their jails of snow.
Waltz with decorum; one step lax or lacking,
One slip on our own graves of many deaths ago,
Betrays us. Ever nearer: the tune of tough ice cracking;

And hands reach out to drag us down below.

Stonehenge

PURER THAN YOU

"This mis-shapen knave,
His mother was a witch; and one so strong
That could control the moon."—*The Tempest,* V, 1.

Small child, mankind, whom aproned eons dandled,
You pranced on saddled truths up this tall hill.
Now to the moon you crow in boastful radar
Yet, pouting, mutilate with pudgy fingers
Your moths and jews and delicate libraries.

Grow, *hybris,* grow till all your toys go mad.
Jack-in-the-box will jump too high one day
And roar, and woe! not Jack must then jump in
The dark and spooky box, and woe! not you
Will dance outside and lock the dreadful latch.
Inside, long hid from you, you'll find that final
Atom of atoms, blazing at your wish
The end you never, never wished. When Kinder-
garten and *Kinder* are no more at all:

Purer than you looms even the Nay Sayer,
That patient fellow who read your heart and waited
Since Eden. He, when all the angels hoped,
Watched God's creation day with folded arms
And smiled aloof how silent, swarthy, proud!

PENELOPE'S LOOM

"Empedocles had spoken of Love and Strife as two forces which respectively gathered and disrupted the elements, so as to carry on between them the Penelope's labor of the world, the one perpetually weaving fresh forms of life and the other perpetually undoing them."—George Santayana.

Earth is the center still, despite our science;
Starlight and sun reach out to stroke her hills.
Sun shouts forth crops in torrid syllables—
But who purrs malediction's midnight lions?

Who hides the earthquake underneath the farm?
Outrageous silver and kind gold of growth
Take turns here; earth, their mænad, lusts for both:
In daytime, she keeps humming-birds from harm,

Is tender to the plum-tree's broken branches,
Feeds yellow tulips from the sallow clay—
But opens up to stars at end of day
And waits in frenzy for their avalanches.

WELL SAID, OLD MOLE

How frail our fists are when they bash or bless
The deadpan idiot emptiness of sky!
In this immortal hoax of Time and Space
(Our creeds and wisecracks equally awry)
We have no solace—no, nor soul—but by
The mortal gesture of a doomed caress:
Man's first and last and honorable reply.
Against the outside Infinite, man weighs
The inwardness within one finite face
And finds all Space less heavy than a sigh
And finds all Time less lingering than *tendresse.*
We are alone and small, and heaven is high;
Quintillion worlds have burst and left no trace;
A murderous star aims straight at where we lie.
And we, all vulnerable and all distress,
Have no brief shield but love and loveliness.
Quick—let me touch your body as we die.

VI

ATHOS AND ASSISI

"Contraries are positive."

(William Blake)

MOUNT ATHOS

The archimandrites in their mountain niches
    Are calling one another;
Like bells in separate steeples, each outstretches
    His bronze tongue to his brother.

On Macedonian hills these abbots kneel
    And rock till hilltops sway.
A goat-herd shudders as his pastures reel:
    "The archimandrites pray!"

Their beds are coffins, and their shirts are shrouds;
    They gash their palms with spears,
While virgin Angels simper from the clouds,
    "Our lovers are so fierce!"

Each archimandrite squats on his own peak
    And bellows at the skies.
Their beards are black and oily, long and sleek,
    And blow towards Paradise.

These burly priests (for patience far too proud)
    Roar out at death's delay;
Their hairy claws are flexed and gouge at God
    To speed his judgment day.

Above Mount Athos, cranes (a migrant swarm
 From Egypt to the Alps)
Are snatched in flight; their blood is guzzled warm
 In wild convulsive gulps;

And then (beyond endurance drunk with lust)
 The archimandrites spill
Their sainthood out: through wombs of clouds they thrust
 Their tautness, tall with Will,

Straight up to heaven—where their earth-love spews.
 Then fluttering Angel squads,
Calmed again, fold their wings, but now their eyes
 Fall when they meet God's.

THREE ODES FROM ASSISI

(crypt of Francis, October, 1945)

I. Exorcism
II. Elegy
III. Incantation

I. EXORCISM

(everybody's two voices)

"To bless"—the patient verb our veins forgot.
  Then "lofty" is more than
A pageant-game? And the sweet tension, the
  Gentleness of
Tremendous enmities is still their need to
  Kiss? And the kindling
Wish to be silvery of tiny snakes is
  A Godward gesture?

> (*And your birds—but O Francis, WHAT of*
>   *the crocodile?*
> *He swims in our veins with a sharp-fanged*
>   *smile.*
> *Would you dance with him in the dark?*
> *Yes, crumbs for the birds—but WHAT for the*
>   *crocodile?*
> *He'll be looking for you in a little while.*
> *Will you meet him alone in the park?*)

The fertilizing ferocity of an idea,
   Hugging whole universes,
Shall teach the pale artists, the rebel-eyed, how to paint
      doves.
   O then, O if only
Tenderness conquer us with the insistent eyes
   That warm without searing,
Then whip-swinging Will, the town bully, is broken by
   The toughness of softness.

   *(It's DOWN with the bully and DOWN with
      the Bad;*
   *But the world is more sad than can ever be
      said,*
   *For a fang that shines whitely can also shine
      red.*
   It's hurrah for ideas and hurrah for the Good;
   *But WHAT of the killer who pants in our
      blood?*
   Will you meet him alone in the wood?)

Then out of that red and brackish and treacherous river
   The irreconcilable crocodile,
Trailing vile mud and fled by all the creatures,
   Crawls to your shrine,
Nuzzling his grotesque, tender, harmful nozzle
   Harmlessly at your startled ankles.
Perhaps even the callous and loveless can yet redeem
      themselves,
   Blessing your blessing.

II. ELEGY TO ALL
SAINTHOOD EVERYWHERE

Now hope, your sipped liqueur and our gulped wine,
Promising us unearned your blessing-power
When you are beautiful in your high blessing-hour,
    Still tricks the loneliness and love
Of hearts which need you, tricks us to your tower.

That little contract which you had with death,
His casual subclause with its fine-print *"dust,"*
Hope hid this from us like amnesia. Now
    We stand here so terribly shattered,
So shattered by death that made your tower a mound.

Hope-swilling on pneumatic cushions, you-ward
    Bus loads of priests and lovers come,
Town-pent and pale as toward a picnic ground,
Begging your blessing like good picnic weather,
    Living your sainthood like a week-end.

They hoped to lounge on kindness as on lawns;
But finding only death's "No Trespass" sign,
    All stand here shy, ungainly now,
Wanting so terribly hard to help you help them,
Wanting to help but never knowing how.

III. INCANTATION

1

Yesterday, a falling rose; tomorrow, a leaf the color of roses.
When a new sacrament is invented, eighth, an eighth,
Its name will be Regret-That-Undoes, an agent, marvelous,
    a magic:
To salvage foundered sincerities from reefs of desolate
    embracing,
To get, to get back
              by praising, by praising.

2

Prayer, delicate,
           the vesper instant:
Fold, fold your hands till the air they prison
Changes to a dove as the great gongs shudder.
Clench it lightly and lightly—vulnerable whiteness;
Love that eluded alleys and implorings
Is pearled in these two oyster-shells of prayer.
"Then adjourn, adjourn," whisper the vespers,
"To the farther side of skies.
After the red rose, the red leaf; but
Always somewhere the white love, wooing
You deathward till your love un-dies."

3

Different:
Here abstractions have contours; here flesh is wraith;
On these cold and warming stones, only solidity throws no
    shadow.
And wrists seem echoes of the chimes they ring.
(Listen, when the high bells ripple the half-light:
Ideas, ideas, the tall ideas dancing.)
This is Assisi, this is
                  a different love and the same;
What twelve years squandered in boulevards and gropings
Was wine poured for
              ghosts. You

Will get it back in Umbria tonight.

VII
AFRICAN CAMPAIGN

AFRICAN AIR

(Dakar, 1943)

The fondling, feline satin of this air
Is Africa. And Africa is air.
And watches us like a perpetual ambush.

> *Everywhere*
> *Purring—and whose*
> *And whose is the invasion?*

Echo of ripeness: thud of unseen fruits.
Tiredest green
From earth's deepest roots.
You heaviness, you
African air.

> *Whose and whose is the invasion?*

Air
Everypurringwhere.

> *Into our shadows Africa is seeping.*

Was that—and whose
And whose is the invasion?—
Was that my
Own
Shadow purring?
You . . . dark . . . African air,
Mere vapor till we sail and think we leave you.

> *Then we discover we are now your air,*
> *And you are we: you breathe us when we breathe.*

ODE TO THRONE AND ALTAR

(inspired by the M.P. chasing me through Algiers)

"Stern Daughter of the Voice of God!
O Duty! . . . Stern Lawgiver! . . . Awful Power!"
—*Wordsworth*

With helmet, scowl, and club, O young M.P.,
Chasing me now along the Rue d'Isly,
You serve bewildered—while I skulk ahead
Casbah-wards past the blacked-out Rue Tancrède—
That ancient grand tradition which hunts down
With equal zest Evil and Harmless Fun.

Your ancestors are not those Grant Wood pairs
You left behind on Kansas rocking-chairs.
You have become your job now, and your own
Are all who did your job once in this town,
Who through these streets chased all who left in lurch
Some form, not substance, of the Throne and Church.

Stone men upon stone horses at the Squares
Bless you—it's these who are your ancestors.
Their glories weigh on you but cannot smother;
You stride between them like an equal brother,
As incorruptible and unforgiving.
You, too, dent skulls for Curfew and Clean Living.

Their very names—take "Maréchal d'Esperey"!—
Are martial music and quaint dignity:
Admiral Pierre; the statue by Dumont
Of Bugeaud, stern proconsul; de Galland,
Lord Mayor, in bas-relief by Bigonet;
Lamy; and Monsignor Lavigerie;

88

France's conquistadors of Africa,
The Duc de Grammont, old proud Lyautey;
Planters and Field Marshals and Cardinals
When throbbing France was still the whole world's pulse.
Against all these—you've found my trail again—
I clutch a dubious "pass for night-work men."

The moon's queer light, which helps me to escape,
Each instant alters your pursuing shape:
A pink-cheeked boyscout playing "cops and robbers,"
A bloodhound with long ears and jowl that slobbers,
A Hollywood portrait of the G. I. G-man,
An atavistic dream of tribal demon.

Bounding, you grow enormous, cosmic-size,
That God of Law in sky above all skies—
Growing up and up and infinitely up—
Who knows each planet's and each sparrow's fall . . .
And yet you hardly look grown-up at all,
A frightened boy who swings a frightening club.

Algiers, 1943

CONVOY FROM NEW YORK

Tune which the hearts and waves and engines beat:
"This is the real thing, this is really it!"
Our troopship has a needed deed to do.
But since love sometimes makes men do deeds better,
May Eisenhower forgive me if for you,
Ellen, only for you I write this letter,
Useless to war as any a seagull feather.

Could my New York, so linked with you, wrench free
From laws of gravity and Albany,
She'd sprout big marvelous wings and soar and bring
Wonders to those who miss her most: to me
Washington Bridge, Fifth Avenue buses, or
At least from West Fourteenth a certain Square
Where memory's white peacock struts as king.

Did those and these arms ever really meet?
Here love's less actual than that other fleet,
The one that's blue and upside down and dances.
Here eyes too wistful in their westward glances,
Will search in vain for ruses to annul
Heart's famous lover-scolded emptinesses
That fill the heart so infinitely full.

The waters touch each face with salt and wonder.
With wonder and steel we touch the water's face.
War is my East; Fourteenth Street is my West.
Before me—if we reach that eastern thunder—
Waits very little rest or longest rest;
Seaweed and equal dozing waits down under;
Both sleeps are cold, and you're in neither place.

And so I write you love leaves stings more aching
Than what the loveless jabbed into the waxen
Shapes of their scorners in old conjurings.
Across all arms stretched out from used-to-be,
Who pulled that blind down? Did I hear glass breaking?
Suddenly I've grown tired as the wings
Of tired seagull lost on open sea.

May, 1943,
S. S. Barnett

VALE FROM CARTHAGE

(Spring, 1944)

I, now at Carthage. He, shot dead at Rome.
Shipmates last May. "And what if one of us,"
I asked last May, in fun, in gentleness,
"Wears doom, like dungarees, and doesn't know?"
He laughed, *"Not see Times Square again?"* The foam,
Feathering across that deck a year ago,
Swept those five words—like seeds—beyond the seas
  Into his future. There they grew like trees;
  And as he passed them there next spring, they laid
  Upon his road of fire their sudden shade.
Though he had always scraped his mess-kit pure
And scrubbed redeemingly his barracks floor,
Though all his buttons glowed their ritual-hymn
Like cloudless moons to intercede for him,
No furlough fluttered from the sky. He will
Not see Times Square—he will not see—he will
Not see Times
    change; at Carthage (while my friend,
Living those words at Rome, screamed in the end)
I saw an ancient Roman's tomb and read
"Vale" in stone. Here two wars mix their dead:
  Roman, my shipmate's dream walks hand in hand
  With yours tonight ("New York again" and
    "Rome"),
  Like widowed sisters bearing water home
  On tired heads through hot Tunisian sand
  In good cool urns, and says, "I understand."
Roman, you'll see your Forum Square no more;
What's left but this to say of any war?

AFRICA AND MY NEW YORK

I.

Too much sugar in these grapes!
Ripeness, which should be born in pain and stillness
Out of the love and struggle of taut wills,
Here comes too facile in a thousand shapes,
With vulgar gaudiness of these too flower-bright hills.
Land without poise, where flabbiness and shrillness
Sweat without toil and spawn without desire,
        Not all your splurge of fruits and wines
Can consecrate your crassness. Trudging higher
        To where the crisp-shelled cacti sprawl
All gangly like a piled-up lobster-haul,
I stop to write these sullen homesick lines,
These futile western fists against your wall.

II.

Only your old are noble, purged by toll
Of parching years; sun spurs them with its stings
But dries this false luxuriance from their soul.
Such are the Marabouts, of whom a prophet sings
That they are dark cocoons of unborn angel-kings.
        Many a wrinkled bigotry of old
        Upon the parchment of these brows is scrolled
And many a fresh aloof lucidity.
        You—Marabout—their gauntest—standing there,
Scorning both Africa and our clean gadget-heavens,
        Assuage this south-incited prayer,
        Assuage, though war's loud nearness deafens,
        My far New York's redemption-plea,
        (New York whose inharmonic self-mocked haste
Is but its hunt for harmony misplaced,
        Whose red-eyed subways charge in wild-bull rage
Only for gentle love's sake); O hear us and assuage:

93

O pagan saints, O frauds whose fraud redeems,
Artist-illiterates, O artists most of all,
Savagely playing art's high game of hatching dreams
    By formal patterns, you from whom sun stole
    All easy lushness as from desert places,
        Teach us your high austere control,
    At first your harshnesses and then your graces:

Give us your cleansing fierceness when you scowl;
Give us the radiancy of your faces.

Souk el Haad,
Algeria, 1943

94

AUTHOR'S NOTE ON
MARABOUTS AND PLANTED POETS

The preceding piece, "Africa And My New York," supplements the theme of "Poet" (on page three), from which in turn the book's title-theme derives. The Marabout parallel implies a word of background. Gentle paupers rich with ferocious redemptions, the Marabouts are individualized and self-disciplined hermits, particularly honored by the Negro and Berber tribes of North Africa. According to one local rumor, their bodies exude so potent an overdose of holiness as to negate the excesses of their African landscape. Thus they dry the vegetation to their own ascetic astringency when buried in the jungles—but sprout forth as oases when interred in the Sahara (as in the recent case of the 99-year-old Marabout Belkacem bel Hadj El-Hamel, forcibly entombed alive in a sandy patch near Bou Saada by the impatient enthusiasm of his adorers).

At a fig market in Hussein Dey, the author asked two camel drivers how many of their people believe in the Marabout miracles. The younger replied, "We all believe, of course." The older, who was blind, added, "That's right: we all believe we believe."

Can it be that the necromancy of the Marabouts "works" (culturally) without being "true" (literally)? Is it perhaps for African-Islamic culture what the poet's incantations are for our Hellas-shaped west? Poetic metaphor as a secularization of "sympathetic magic": with Koran or with rhyming-dictionary, to tame each thunderous force of nature by knowing its secret unnameable Name and saying it in the ritual of rhythm. Buried Marabout, or planted poet: the God-intoxicated exorcizer of demons, or the Word-sobered exorcizer of clichés. Like the court jester and the patent-medicine quack, both the saint-charlatan

95

of the east and the rhyme-manipulator of the west are modern relics of the prehistoric culture-hero,* the liberating "transvaluator of all values," the martyred witch, the sacred clown.

Wintering in the tomb-womb of the fertile grave, the culture-hero returns from exile as from a psychological hibernation. To believers in his ambiguous magic, this exile may be "death," Hell, the Orphic descent to Hades, Beowulf's harrowing in Grendel's lair, the Eliotine waste land, the night where you lose your "shadow," or even the alleged "escapism" and seeming detachment of esthete's ivory tower. The returner returns in springtime (fertility time, Easter-bunny time), or in timeless legend, or in some Eternal Recurrence (some "haven't I been here before?" time). And above all, he returns as law-giver and as healer: like the song-quickening Orpheus or the soil-quickening Osiris; like the roamers Kilroy and Ulysses and Icarus, man's three redeemers from suburbia; like some hibernating totem animal of American Indians, like our own current folklore of the "shadowless" groundhog whose hibernation brings spring, or like that bear whom the hairy Ainus of the Pacific annually crucify and love.

To be a spring-bearer is never a safe job. For example, the Shilluk herdsmen of the Sudan cannily kill (plant) their priest-king before he loses his good health; he "must not be allowed to become ill or senile lest, with his diminishing vigor, the cattle should sicken and fail to bear their increase and the crops should wither in the fields."† One is reminded of the *Waste Land* question, "That corpse you planted . . . has it begun to sprout?," to which all

---

*The word "culture-hero" is borrowed, somewhat warily, from the lamentable jargon of anthropology. It is used above to define those Promethean alchemists, conjuring civilization out of savagery, whom legend records or invents.

†B. Z. and C. G. Seligman, *The Pagan Tribes of the Nilotic Sudan,* London, 1932; page 90.

the vulnerable glibness of our cities can only answer, "Nope!"

Shelley's apparently unrealistic aphorism (poets as mankind's "unacknowledged legislators") makes pretty good sense—provided the stress is on "unacknowledged": like Kilroy, the planted poet also "was here" and was everywhere; but the point is that nobody has really seen either of them. *Do they exist?* If not, then it is hardly a case of "so much the worse for them"; it is so much the worse for existence. For their patterns, like the equally non-existent universals of Plato, may be daily molding our meaningless existence into meaning.

No need for such humorless and pretentious nineteenth-century romanticism as O'Shaughnessy's "three with a new song's measure / Can trample an empire down." Excursions of the visceral and irrational into the prose realm of politics and economics are either silly or sinister. The poet as culture-hero has more basic things to trample down than empires, unless it be the Empire of the Id. Rejecting both unrigorousness and *rigor mortis,* both the formlessness of bohemia and the formalities of philistia, the poet imposes form upon nature, humanism upon the inhuman. That this esthetic triumph may involve more terror than prettiness, or more irony than Lofty Sentiments, is suggested by the poems "The Killer and the Dove," "Poet," "Kilroy," "Dolce Ossessione," "A Walk on Snow," "Ballad of the Jollie Gleeman," and the "Proöimion" of the "Six Theological Cradle-Songs."

Culture-heroes are not the same as culture-hounds. Beauty is not the same as noble-browed Beautiful Souls. Its fierceness-and-decorum is too bitter for them and too outrageous. Their reaction recalls those three words of Rinaldino, the highminded hero of Clipwell's Andorran tragedy:*

*Amadeus Clipwell, *Murther and Lust in Olde Andorra,* Act One Scene 83.

97

REGINALDO: Hush!, 'tis Sir Hex, the Master of this
mansion;
His wits are out againe from too much
musick.
(Once at Damascus he converst with
birds.)
Meseemes he'll cudgel us until we chirp.
(This happens ev'ry Spring).

RINALDINO: Monstrous! O monstrous!

VIII

REVERENCE

★ ❦ ★

"Not magnitude, not lavishness,
But Form—the Site;
Not innovating wilfulness,
But reverence for the Archetype."

(Herman Melville)

AFFIRMATIONS

(I, II, III)

I. GLADNESS ODE

Because you made me glad, I was the net.
"Why do you haunt me?" asked the midnight lake.
    "To fish," I said, "that rounded fire.
      Am not afraid to fall."

No, though that halo moved and moved and moved,
It could not hide from me for all its slyness.
    (Beneath the waters warningly
      Moon's Icaruses sprawl.)

High watchers glowed their pity on the lake:
"To wear a mirrored circle like a crown,
    Is it for this the young men drown?"
      But I, being net, must haul.

Before you made me glad, I feared such splashing;
Futile invoker then: "Dive me-ward, moon."
    But now it's I who dive defiant
      Cold curves like a ball.

The lake sang out in grace-notes scrawled by stars.
I was the net, and all my strands were glad.
    I pulled the moon out of the water;
      It wasn't heavy at all.

II. IN DEFENSE OF GLADNESS

Not enough: the moonward
Arms of "I want, I want." Our least futile
Gesture, bold and debonair, is it not to
Touch, to clutch? But life we catch only

In reflection, in reflected blazing.
And if for this we need an ally, then—
Not art after all? Love? Possibly love?
"Infirm of purpose, O Muse, poor cat i' the adage,"

Says love, "give *me* the daggers!"

III. THE KILLER AND THE DOVE

This poacher, for an old obsession's sake,
Still stalks dove-whiteness, mirrored in his lake.
True wings shine overhead, too high to capture,
Moon of his blood and feather of his rapture.

"Help, holy dove; I'm masked in earthbound meshes;
Fly down, You vowel of God, You first-born Word.
(Then I'll fly up, yes I, less white a bird.)
Free me; I sink as if my feet were fishes.

"I sink; am I unwelcome in your welkin?
Reach down from sky and rip at my disguising:
Be knot, but first be knife.
                    . . . Beware up there; I'm rising
To You—to You!—
                    to pounce:
                            my name is falcon."

THE NEW GUEST PROMENADES
WITH A FEATHER IN HIS CAP
(for a christening)

"That sunset tourists hike so far to visit,
Where shall I trail it and how recognize?"
  The famous view that's viewing you is ice.

"I'll toss you all the tips your palms solicit.
Which way?"
        Young master, anywhere you wish it.
    You'll need no alpenstock. Your cab—dismiss it.
    Only your skin, sir; try it on for size.

"Guide, stop the sun, please. And be more explicit.
I run and run; the sunset faster flies."
    You'll sleep with it the night you catch and kiss it.
    But what's the hurry? Waiting will suffice:
    Say, sixty years . . . then any bait will fish it.

"Come, fellow, come; show me that paradise."
    Your heels will see it if you scan the skies.

"Old fool, what Baedeker can I elicit,
Which final inn to answer my where-is-it?"
    We natives always say: 'You just can't miss it,'
    Not even if you shut your eyes.

I AM DYING, EGYPT, DYING

The first letter I ever got: "Dere crybaby, I'le
Mete you behind the jym and bust your jaw." While
The weather was good, we hiked maybe a mile
In New Jersey, yelling "RIGHT, LEFT" in single file;

Then back by ferry, yawning all the way.
("Progressive education means fooling around with clay.")
Or the time the piano teacher made Joanie play
Sur la glace à Sweet Briar before the whole (they

Were grinning; this was in the fourth grade) pew.
In biology lab, I never saw anything (you
May consider this a Confession) through
That microscope, but I had to pretend to.

My hold on Remember will skid (HELP, HELP) when
    I die.
So call it "Elegy On My Own Self" (WHO'S THAT?) by
Which I mean the specialness of (YOU!) any guy.
Or—call it "Maybe Survival" because (LOOKIT) my

Fading hand holds these unfading photos of "I."

CRASS TIMES REDEEMED
BY DIGNITY OF SOULS

(For Ted Spencer. Lines in memory of the humanistic
ideals of my brother, Corporal George S. Viereck, Jr.,
killed in action by the Nazis in 1944)

i

The music of the dignity of souls
Molds every note I hum and hope to write.
I long to tell the Prince of aureoles—
Groper-in-clay and breather-into-dolls,
Kindler of suns, and chord that spans our poles—
What goading reverence His tunes incite.
Then lips whose only sacrament is speech,
Sing Him the way the old unbaptized night
Dreads and
        needs and
            lacks and
                loves the light.
May yet when slick with poise I overreach,
When that high ripening slowness I impeach,
Awe of that music jolt me home contrite:

O harshness of the dignity of souls.

The tenderness of dignity of souls
Sweetens our cheated gusto and consoles.
It shades love's lidless eyes like parasols
And tames the earthquake licking at our soles.
Re-tunes the tensions of the flesh we wear.
Forgives the dissonance our triumphs blare.
And maps the burrows of heart's buried lair
Where furtive furry Wishes hide like moles.
O hear the kind voice, hear it everywhere
(It sings, it sings, it conjures and cajoles)
Prompting us shyly in our half-learnt rôles.
It sprouts the great chromatic vine that lolls
In small black petals on our music scrolls
(It flares, it flowers—it quickens yet controls).
It teaches dance-steps to this uncouth bear
Who hops and stumbles in our skin and howls.

The weight that tortures diamonds out of coals
Is lighter than the skimming hooves of foals
Compared to one old heaviness our souls
Hoist daily, each alone, and cannot share:
To-be-awake, to sense, to-be-aware.
Then even the dusty dreams that clog our skulls,
The rant and thunder of the storm we are,
The sunny silences our prophets hear,
The rainbow of the oil upon the shoals,
The crimes and Christmases of creature-lives,
And all pride's barefoot tarantelle on knives
Are but man's search for dignity of souls.

The searcher for the market price of souls,
Seth the Accuser with the donkey head,
Negation's oldest god, still duns the dead
For these same feathery Egyptian tolls—
But now, bland haggler, deprecates his quest
(The devil proving devils can't exist).
His boutonnière is a chic asphodel;
He makes Id's whirlpool seem a wishing-well,
Reflecting crowns to outstretched beggar-bowls.
No horns, no claws; that cheap exotic phase
Belonged to his first, gauche, bohemian days.
The nice, the wholesome, and the commonplace
Are Trilbys he manipulates in jest
Till their dear wheedlings subtly swerve our goals:—

MASK ONE: an honest, cleancut, sporting face
Such as will cheer for wrong with righteous grace,
Hiking in shorts through tyranny's Tyrols.
MASK TWO: a round and basking babyface
Distracts our souls, so archly does it beg,
Upblinking like a peevish pink poached-egg.
THIRD MASK: his hide-out is that ageing face
Which waits for youth in mirrors like an ambush
And lives our ardent "when"s as yawning "if"s
And, puffing corncobs, drawls between two whiffs,
"Why stick your neck out? Nonsense never pays!"
And rips our aspirations like a thornbush.
Unmasked on tombs by shrieking hieroglyphs,
Seth was his true—his hungry—donkey face,
Nibbling our souls as if their groans were grass,
This grazer on the dignity of souls.

He, the huge bridegroom of all servile souls,
Swaps little jokes with little envious trolls
To snuff the radiance of tragedy
And vend us Pleasure, which turns out to be
An optimistic mechanized despair.
O hear the glib voice, hear it everywhere
(It shouts, it shouts, it cadges and cajoles).
It feeds the earthquake fawning at our soles.
It hands out free omnipotence as doles.
Replaces tall towns with still deeper holes.
To make us God, needs just one hair's-breadth more.

The Agents said, "All ungregarious souls
Are priggish outlaws, stubborn Seminoles."
In Confidential Chats and Friendly Strolls,
They warned us each:
                    "You are alone, you are
The last, you are the lost—O flee—you are
The straggling warrior of the lost last war
To vindicate the dignity of souls."

We answered: "*Tell the Prince who brays at souls,*
Your long-eared Lord with thornless crowns to sell,
That all his halos have a sulphur smell;
And though they flash like flying orioles
Or lure like bonfires on mountain knolls,
These gaudy girandoles are
                               blackness still."

Torn out of blackness, soon to choke on black,
Leaning on nothingness before and back,
Tight-lashed to lies by veins and nerves and Will,
My life is darkness. Yet I live to tell
How shimmering, how gaily freedom prowls
In flesh that guards its consciousness of souls.
Then love that gives and gives and loves the more,
Frees us the way the good and daily light
Heals and
            shreds and
                          liberates the night.
Though blinking—burning—shivering in the white
Blaze that each dust-heap blest with speech extols,
May every dark and kindled "I" revere
In every "you" that selfsame fire-core,
In every soul the soul of all our souls.